MOTORBIKES

Debbie Croft

Contents

What Are Motorbikes?

Motorbikes are vehicles that people use to travel from place to place. Most motorbikes have two wheels, similar to bicycles, but they have engines so they do not need to be pedalled.

Usually, motorbikes are ridden by just one person. But a passenger can also sit on the bike behind the rider.

Think and Talk About ...

Both the rider and a passenger on a motorbike must wear a helmet.

A motorbike rider with a passenger races across the countryside.

A rider travels along the Pan-American Highway in Peru.

Think and Talk About ...

Motorbikes can be dangerous to ride in the winter when the road may be covered with ice or snow.

Headlights on motorbikes make riders visible to drivers, especially in bad weather.

Motorbikes are not as heavy as cars, so many of them can be ridden very fast. The riders do not have much protection from the wind or rain. This makes motorbikes difficult to ride in bad weather.

Motorbike riders can move quickly through traffic on their way to work.

There are a wide range of designs of motorbikes, because they are used for different purposes. Some are used for riding long distances. Some people use motorbikes to travel to and from work, and others use motorbikes for riding on tracks that are not on public roads.

A motorbike rider enjoys the freedom of the open road.

A rider takes part in an enduro race in Predappio, Italy.

There are three main groups of motorbikes: street bikes, off-road bikes and bikes that can be used for both on- and off-road activities.

Street bikes include standard bikes, cruisers, sports bikes and touring bikes. There are various types of off-road motorbikes. They are used for events such as **motocross** and **enduro** racing. Trail bikes and trial bikes are other types of off-road motorbikes.

It is not legal to ride most off-road bikes on public roads. However, some motorbikes are built so they can be used off road, but they are also legal and comfortable to ride on the streets.

Street Bikes

Street bikes are motorbikes with grooved tyres. They are designed for riding on sealed roads. Most street bikes can be ridden at speeds up to 160 kilometres per hour. Some can reach speeds greater than 200 kilometres per hour. There are several different types of street bikes.

Standard Motorbikes

Standard motorbikes are basic motorbikes that are ideal for beginner riders. They do not have really powerful engines, and they are not as expensive to buy as some other types of bikes. The rider of a standard motorbike can sit comfortably in an upright position because the foot pegs are directly below the seat.

Street bikes are convenient for riding around the city, and they are easy to park.

A cruiser motorbike is useful for a comfortable trip when the rider is not in a hurry.

Cruisers

On cruiser motorbikes, the rider sits with their feet in front of the seat and their hands up high. They sit up straight, or lean slightly backwards. This position is more comfortable at low speeds, because the force of the wind at high speeds can make the rider become tired very quickly.

A cruiser does not go around corners as well as other types of bikes. There is not much **clearance** between the ground and the bottom of the bike.

Sports Bikes

Sports bikes can reach high speeds very quickly. They are known for their speed, braking and cornering on the roads. They have powerful engines and lightweight frames. These bikes have "fairings". A fairing is a shell over the frame of the bike that reduces the force of the wind against the bike and its rider. A sports bike has a windscreen that helps to protect the rider from strong winds or heavy rain.

Think and Talk About …

Sports bikes have high-performance brake pads to keep riders safe if they have to slow down or stop suddenly.

It takes practice and training to ride a sports bike at high speed on the racetrack.

A rider explores the Pacific coast of California, the USA, on a touring bike.

Touring Bikes

Touring bikes are specially designed for travelling long distances. They have large fuel tanks so riders can go a long way before they have to stop to refuel. A touring bike gives the rider an upright, relaxed seating position. A touring bike also has a seat for a passenger and storage space for luggage.

Off-Road Motorbikes

Off-road motorbikes are also known as dirt bikes. They have been designed for a variety of off-road activities. These motorbikes are usually simpler and lighter than street bikes. There is more space between the ground and the bike, too, because the bikes are often ridden over rough and uneven ground.

A rider performs a jump on an off-road bike.

An on- and off-road bike is ideal for the daily commute, and for having fun.

On- and Off-Road Motorbikes

On- and off-road motorbikes are legal to ride on the streets, but are also designed to be ridden off road. Basically, they are built like dirt bikes, but they are fitted with lights, mirrors, indicators and other instruments.

An on- and off-road bike can be used for enduro racing.

Motorbikes for Specific Events

Type of Motorbike	Description
Motocross Bikes	Motocross bikes are raced on short, off-road tracks. In these races, riders have to jump obstacles at high speeds. A motocross bike has a small fuel tank to reduce the total weight of the bike.
Enduro Bikes	In enduro motorbike racing, riders compete over a very long course, sometimes through desert landscapes, which may take between one and six days to complete. Some enduro bikes have been altered so they can be legally ridden on the streets. They have horns, lights and number plates.
Trail Bikes	Trail bikes can be ridden on road and for **recreational** off-road riding. Trail bikes are usually not as well-equipped as other types of motorbikes, because they are not used for competition.
Trial Bikes	Trial riding is a form of off-road competition. It tests the skills of balance and **precision**, rather than speed. A trial bike has a lightweight frame with a small engine. During the trial, the riders stand on the foot pegs, so some bikes do not have seats.
Track Racing Bikes	Track racing bikes compete in high-speed oval racing. These bikes have only two gears, and they have no brakes. They are designed to make only left-hand turns, because all the races are run in an anti-clockwise direction.

Think and Talk About . . .

Motocross bikes are designed without lights and mirrors to keep their weight as low as possible.

Motocross riders race through the dust.

Think and Talk About . . .

Trial bike riding is all about negotiating obstacles rather than riding at high speeds.

Antoni Bou, world champion trial bike rider, competes in Barcelona, Spain.

Riding Motorbikes

Riding a motorbike requires attention to safety, just like driving a car. Motorbikes can travel as fast as or faster than cars, but they do not have as many safety features. A motorbike does not have a frame around the rider or seatbelts, and is not as stable as a car because it has only two wheels. This means riders must take extra care to be safe when they are riding.

Think and Talk About . . .

Many countries have laws about motorbike helmets, to help keep riders safe.

Motorbike riders share busy roads with cars, buses and other vehicles.

The following safety tips can help riders to be safe on their motorbikes.

Every rider should:

- wear a well-fitted helmet every time they ride the bike.
- wear suitable safety clothing. This includes clothing that has long sleeves and long pants for extra protection in case the rider slides along the surface of the road. Many riders wear leather jackets and pants that have pads on the elbows and knees.
- wear shoes that have low heels and strong soles that protect the rider's ankles. This makes it easier to balance the bike when the rider slows down or stops.
- take extra care in rainy weather, because wet roads can be very slippery.
- leave enough space between their bike and other vehicles on the road. This will give the rider time to slow down or stop to avoid a collision.
- ride according to their own skill level – they should ride only in situations where they know they will be safe.
- attend a motorbike training course before they ride on the roads. These courses teach riders how to respond in an emergency, how to avoid unsafe situations and how to maintain their motorbike.

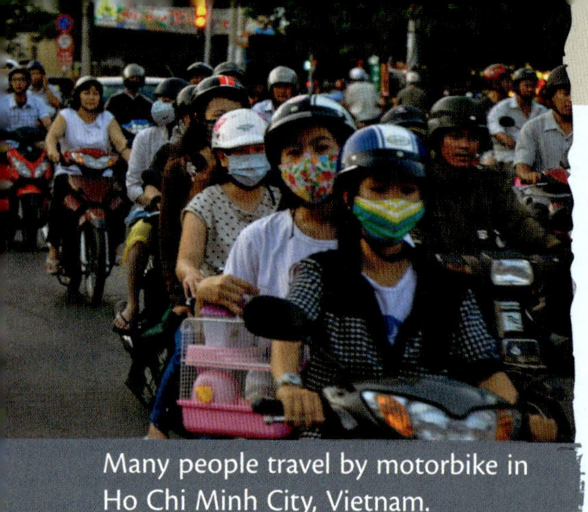

Many people travel by motorbike in Ho Chi Minh City, Vietnam.

In **developing countries**, motorbikes are mostly used for transport. They are cheaper than cars to buy and they cost less to operate. Usually, motorbikes can travel a long way on a small amount of fuel.

In **developed countries**, motorbikes are mainly used for recreation, or as a hobby. Some people join motorbike clubs so they can take long rides with other people who also enjoy riding.

On weekends, groups of people who all own a particular brand of motorbike can often be seen riding through the countryside. Usually, they arrange to have breaks or stop for lunch at **designated** points. Then, they continue their ride, either returning along the same road, or perhaps completing a loop to arrive back at their starting point.

Riding up a mountain pass in Austria is a scenic day out for members of a motorbike club.

Motorbikes are a convenient and affordable form of transport for many people. Different types of motorbikes can be used for travel and recreational activities. However, motorbike riders have less protection than people travelling by car, and bad weather can make riding dangerous. Therefore, riders need to exercise a high degree of caution at all times.

Motorbikes have developed in comfort and speed since the early 1900s.

This woman is dressed for safety as she rides on a country road in California, the USA.

An Unforgettable Day!

After what seemed like a lifetime, the day of the first round in the International Race Series had finally arrived! The main race was about to begin. Dad and I quickly found our seats in the grandstand, where we had an excellent view of the track.

This year's championship was expected to be the best ever. There were several riders who had the potential to win the series, so I knew the racing would be spectacular to watch.

Usually, I followed the racing closely on television, as the riders travelled to different **circuits** around the world. But I knew that watching this first race of the season live would be far more exciting!

The riders took their places on the starting grid. It was thrilling just to hear the rumble of the bike engines as the machines idled into position.

As soon as all the bikes were steady, the red light came on, and the five-second countdown to the start began. Then the red light went out and the race was officially underway.

The start was a surge of power, as the riders revved their bikes and lunged off the line. I could feel the stands shudder under my feet from the **vibrations** of the bikes on the track. The rider in **pole position** led the race up the hill towards the first corner. The bikes disappeared in a single line around the bend, with only a split second separating the first few riders.

Soon, the bikes came into view again on the far side of the track.
In the distance, I could hear the smooth sound of the engines as the bikes **accelerated** along the back straight. This was so much better than watching the race on television!

For about twenty laps, the riders zigzagged their way around the course, changing leaders on almost every lap. The bikes whizzed past us, blurred by their incredible speed. The burnt smell of **high-octane fuel** hung in the air – something that had been missing when I watched races on television.

On the twenty-fifth lap, the **marshals** suddenly waved their yellow flags. The riders immediately slowed, and circled the track at a less frantic pace. At the end of **pit straight**, one of the riders had clipped the back of the bike in front of him, causing them both to skid off into the gravel bed at the side of the track. It was clear that no one was injured, as both riders were soon on their feet.

The safety car was **deployed** and led the remaining riders in single file until the two bikes had been loaded onto trailers and returned to the pits. For those riders, their day was over. I felt so disappointed for the teams who now had to be content to watch the other riders battle it out for a **podium position**.

When the action restarted, the riders were quickly back to racing speed. Their top-of-the-line racing bikes chewed up the laps, and all too soon, the race was in its final stage. There was only one lap to go and there were three bikes challenging for the number one position!

At lap record speed, the bikes rounded the final corner into pit straight. The rider at the front of the pack, no doubt feeling the pressure, went out a little too wide on the track. The second-placed rider seized the opportunity to slip past and take the lead. The crowd went wild!

17
17
7
7

Mechanics and pit crew members from each of the teams were standing near the pit wall, waiting for the final result to unfold. As the leading rider sped across the finish line, the marshal waved the chequered flag, indicating that the race was over and the winner had been declared.

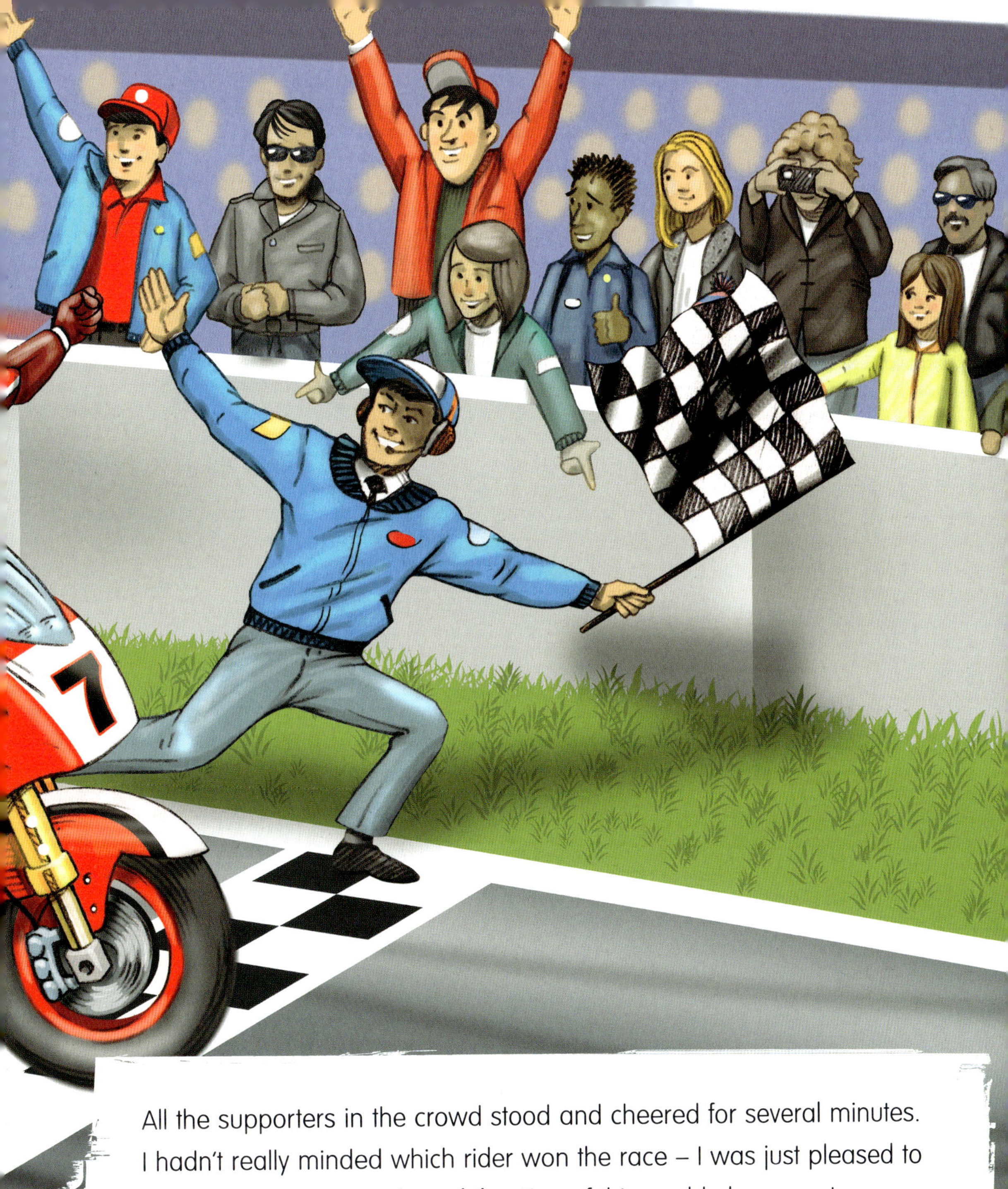

All the supporters in the crowd stood and cheered for several minutes. I hadn't really minded which rider won the race – I was just pleased to be able to experience the **exhilaration** of this world-class event.

It was several minutes before we could make our way down through the crowd to where the winner was waiting to be interviewed. His crew extended hearty congratulations, as he took off his helmet and unzipped his leather race suit.

At the presentation after the race, the winner seemed to be a very humble champion. He praised his team of mechanics and the hundreds of people involved in organising the race. Then he complimented the other riders on their skill and sporting behaviour. He was presented with the winner's trophy by a representative of the event's major **sponsor**.

All too quickly, the winner was whisked away to the media room, where a television crew was set up for a live **press conference**.

It had been an unforgettable day. I knew that from now on, every time I settled in to watch a race on television at home, my mind would automatically return to the elation I felt at this moment. It had been such an amazing day.

Glossary

accelerated *(verb)*	increased speed
circuits *(noun)*	circular racing tracks, or different races in a season
clearance *(noun)*	the amount of space between the bottom of a vehicle and the road or track underneath it
deployed *(verb)*	sent out from a base for a special purpose
designated *(adjective)*	chosen, selected or specified
developed countries *(noun)*	countries where people have high standards of living
developing countries *(noun)*	countries where people have low standards of living
enduro *(noun)*	a long distance, off-road motorbike race
exhilaration *(noun)*	a feeling of being alive and excited
high-octane fuel *(noun)*	good-quality fuel that helps engines run powerfully
marshals *(noun)*	people in charge of a racetrack
motocross *(noun)*	a short distance, off-road motorbike race
pit straight *(noun)*	the straight part of a racetrack just before the finish line
podium position *(noun)*	a place among the first three
pole position *(noun)*	the front position in the starting line-up
precision *(noun)*	accuracy or exactness in doing something
press conference *(noun)*	when a famous person gives a media interview
recreational *(adjective)*	something that is done for fun or entertainment
sponsor *(noun)*	a company that pays for a sporting event in exchange for being able to advertise at the event
vibrations *(noun)*	shaking movements

Index